The Story of Mom

A guided memoir and family keepsake book

BroadStreet
PUBLISHING

BroadStreet Publishing Group, LLC.
Savage, Minnesota, USA
Broadstreetpublishing.com

The Story of Mom

9781424572021

Typesetting and design by Garborg Design Works | garborgdesign.com
Compiled and edited by Michelle Winger | literallyprecise.com

Printed in China.

26 27 28 29 30 31 32 7 6 5 4 3 2 1

For my children—

the greatest gifts of my life.

May these pages remind you

of where you come from,

and how deeply you are loved.

Dear Loved One,

This book is an invitation. It's a place for me to gather the memories, stories, lessons, and dreams that have shaped my life. Within these pages you'll find both the little details and the big milestones: the things I loved, the work I pursued, the people I cherished, and the wisdom I've gathered along the way.

I created this as a way to preserve my story for you—not just the facts, but the feelings, the laughter, the struggles, and the values that made me who I am. My hope is that as you read, you will see not only where I've been, but also the hope I've carried at every stage of my journey.

This is not meant to be perfect or polished. Some stories may trail off, some memories may be incomplete, and some answers may surprise you. But together they weave the tapestry of a life: a story of faith, resilience, joy, and love.

I hope that in these words you find connection, comfort, and maybe even a little inspiration. Most of all, I hope you will always know how deeply you are loved.

With all my heart,

Contents

Every story
begins somewhere,
and mine began
with the simple
joys and lessons
of being a child.

CHAPTER 1
Childhood

SIBLING
SIBLING
FATHER
ME
SIBLING
MOTHER
SIBLING

GRANDFATHER
GRANDMOTHER
GRANDFATHER
GRANDMOTHER
Family tree

"Let the little children come to me and do not hinder them, for to such belongs the kingdom of heaven."
MATTHEW 19:14 ESV

Where My Story Begins

When were you born and where? What details do you know about your birth?

How did your parents choose your name? Does it have a special meaning?

What nickname were you given as a child? Who gave it to you?

What was your hometown like?

What is one of your very first memories?

What did your first home look like, and who lived there with you?

What relatives lived nearby or were part of your early life?

What toys did you love most as a child?

Did you have a favorite blanket, stuffed animal, or comfort item?

What made you feel safe when you were little?

What things frightened you?

If you had siblings, what were their names and what was the age difference?

Did you share a room, or did you have your own? What did it look like?

What was your relationship with your siblings like?

What family traditions do you remember the most?

The best thing about
the future is that it comes
one day at a time.

ABRAHAM LINCOLN

What kinds of outings or adventures did your family go on when you were young?

What were mealtimes like in your family?

How did your family celebrate birthdays?

What chore or responsibility did you especially like or dislike?

Who were your earliest playmates? Who was your best friend growing up?

Did you play mostly inside or outside? What games did you play?

What forts, treehouses, or secret hiding spots did you make for yourself?

What toys, books, or games do you remember most vividly?

What songs, shows, or movies captured your imagination?

If you had pets, what were they, and what were their names?

What was your proudest achievement as a child?

What kind of mischief or trouble did you get into?

What made you laugh the hardest?

Who did you look up to or admire most, and why?

What do you think shaped "little you" the most?

What birthday celebration or gift stands out, and what made it so memorable?

What childhood memory is your favorite, and why?

Share the favorite memory you have of your mom and of your dad.

Never be afraid
to trust an unknown
future to a known God.
CORRIE TEN BOOM

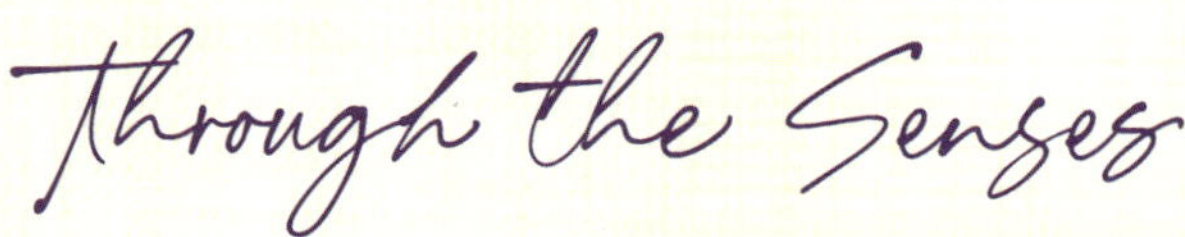

What was the view from your childhood bedroom?

What everyday sounds remind you of your childhood?

What smell instantly transports you back to your childhood?

What was your favorite meal, snack, or treat as a child?

How did you receive comfort?

If you could capture the feeling of your childhood in one word, what would it be, and why?

Childlike Faith

Jesus called for the children, saying, "Let the little children come to me. Don't stop them, because the kingdom of God belongs to people who are like these children."

LUKE 18:16 NCV

Children, in their innocence and faith, do not have the chip on their shoulders that adults do. Adults may hear the gospel and balk, unwilling to believe it's true. Children accept it more readily. If the gospel didn't sound too good to be true, it wouldn't represent the fullness of God's love. Dare to believe it as a child believes dependable adults. God is a good father.

Childlike faith means taking God at his word and being overcome with wonder at the simplest of things. It means carrying a measure of joyful awe wherever you go. Let go of your need to be overly mature or to understand everything in the moment. Learn to enjoy life a little more, and incorporate delightful innocence back into your life.

When you think back to your childhood, what characteristics would you like to carry into your relationship with God?

May the laughter of childhood echo in your heart, reminding you of innocence and joy.

The classroom taught me facts, but life itself taught me wisdom.

CHAPTER 2

Education

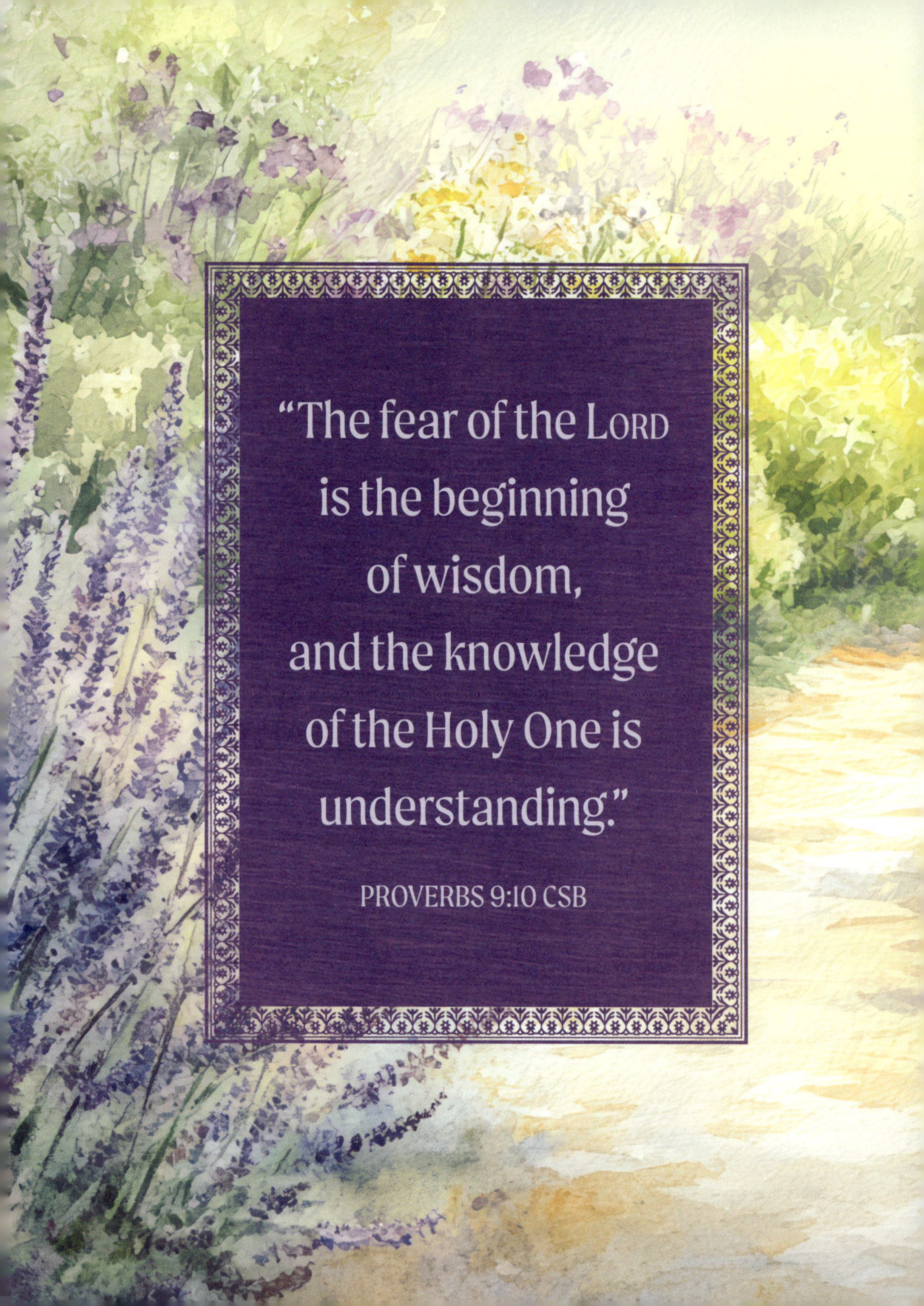
"The fear of the LORD
is the beginning
of wisdom,
and the knowledge
of the Holy One is
understanding."
PROVERBS 9:10 CSB

My Schoolhouse Story

What do you remember about your first day of school?

Who was your first teacher and what stands out about them?

How did you get to school? What do you remember about that?

What subjects did you enjoy the most and why?

Which subjects did you find difficult?

What was your favorite lunch?

Who were your closest friends during your early school years?

What field trips or class events stand out to you?

How big was your high school and what was it like?

What else did you participate in at school?

What did you do with friends after school?

What rewards or recognition did you receive during your school years?

What important lesson did you learn about friendship in your teen years?

Did you ever face peer pressure, and how did you handle it?

What mistakes did you make during these years that helped you grow?

There are far, far better things ahead than any we leave behind.

C.S. LEWIS

What coach, youth leader, or counselor guided you in an important way?

What did you learn about independence and responsibility during high school?

If you could give your teenage-self advice, what would it be?

What's something you're glad you tried, and why?

What are you thankful you avoided, and why?

How did you decide what college to attend (or not attend)?

Where did you live during this time, and what was memorable about it?

How did you manage responsibilities like money, schedules, and studying?

What did you study, and why did you choose that path?

Did you ever consider a completely different education path?

What life lesson came from a mistake you made in your late teens or early twenties?

When did you truly feel like an adult for the first time?

Who influenced you the most during your college or training years?

What values or principles were solidified for you during this stage of life?

What did your teenage and young adult years teach you about resilience and hope?

What was the biggest challenge you faced in your education, and what did it teach you about yourself?

What might you have done differently in school had you known then what you know now?

What high school teacher, coach, or other mentor made the biggest impact on you, and why?

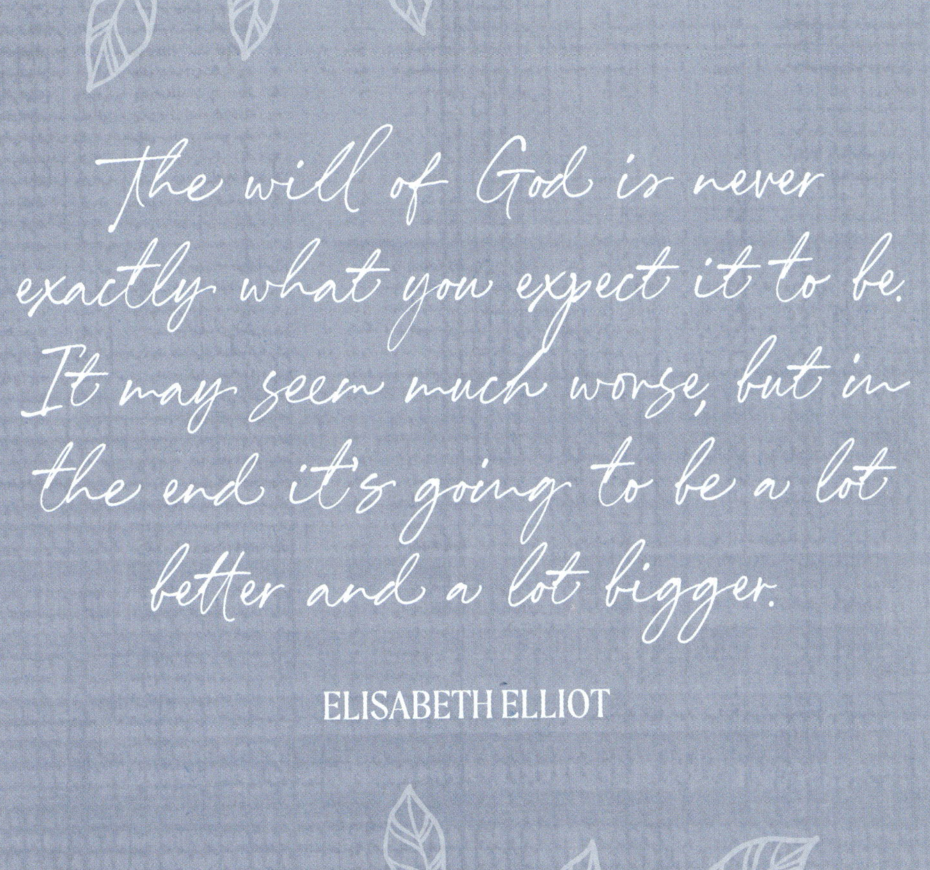
The will of God is never exactly what you expect it to be. It may seem much worse, but in the end it's going to be a lot better and a lot bigger.
ELISABETH ELLIOT

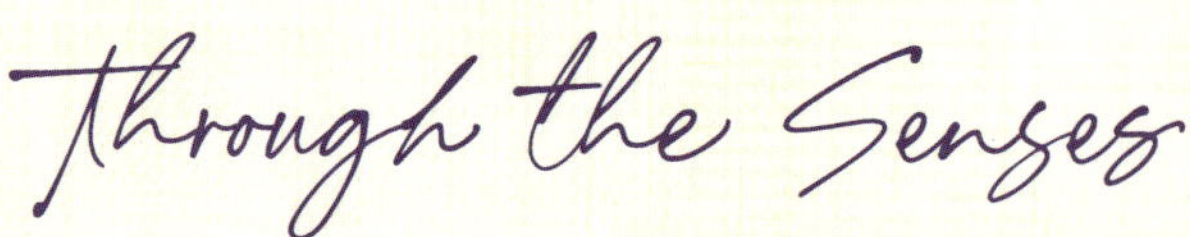

What style of clothing did you and your friends wear in your school years?

What soundtrack or song defines your high school life?

What scent instantly takes you back to those days?

What food instantly reminds you of study sessions or hangouts?

What did you learn by doing with your hands rather than just listening?

What moment as a student made you feel most alive?

Spiritually Educated

We continually ask God to fill you with the knowledge of his will through all the wisdom and understanding that the Spirit gives, so that you may live a life worthy of the Lord and please him in every way: bearing fruit in every good work, growing in the knowledge of God.

COLOSSIANS 1:9-10 NIV

We are wired to look at education as a means to an end; once we receive our qualification we can head into our careers and earn a decent living. God's knowledge, however, isn't about what we can gain in life but about what we can gain in relationship with him. Knowing God doesn't require a PhD; it requires following Jesus through the guidance of his Holy Spirit.

You won't please God by meeting the right requirements, but he will be pleased with a heart that acknowledges his way above your own. Rely on the Holy Spirit and notice how you are able to continually seek wisdom in all you do. Let growth take place one day at a time. When you are confused about your life, purpose, or relationships, ask God for understanding. He will fill you with the knowledge you need for each moment.

How have you become spiritually educated over the course of your life?

May every lesson
learned become
a steppingstone
toward wisdom
and grace.

Through the work of my hands and the labor of my days, I learned perseverance, purpose, and provision.

CHAPTER 3

Work

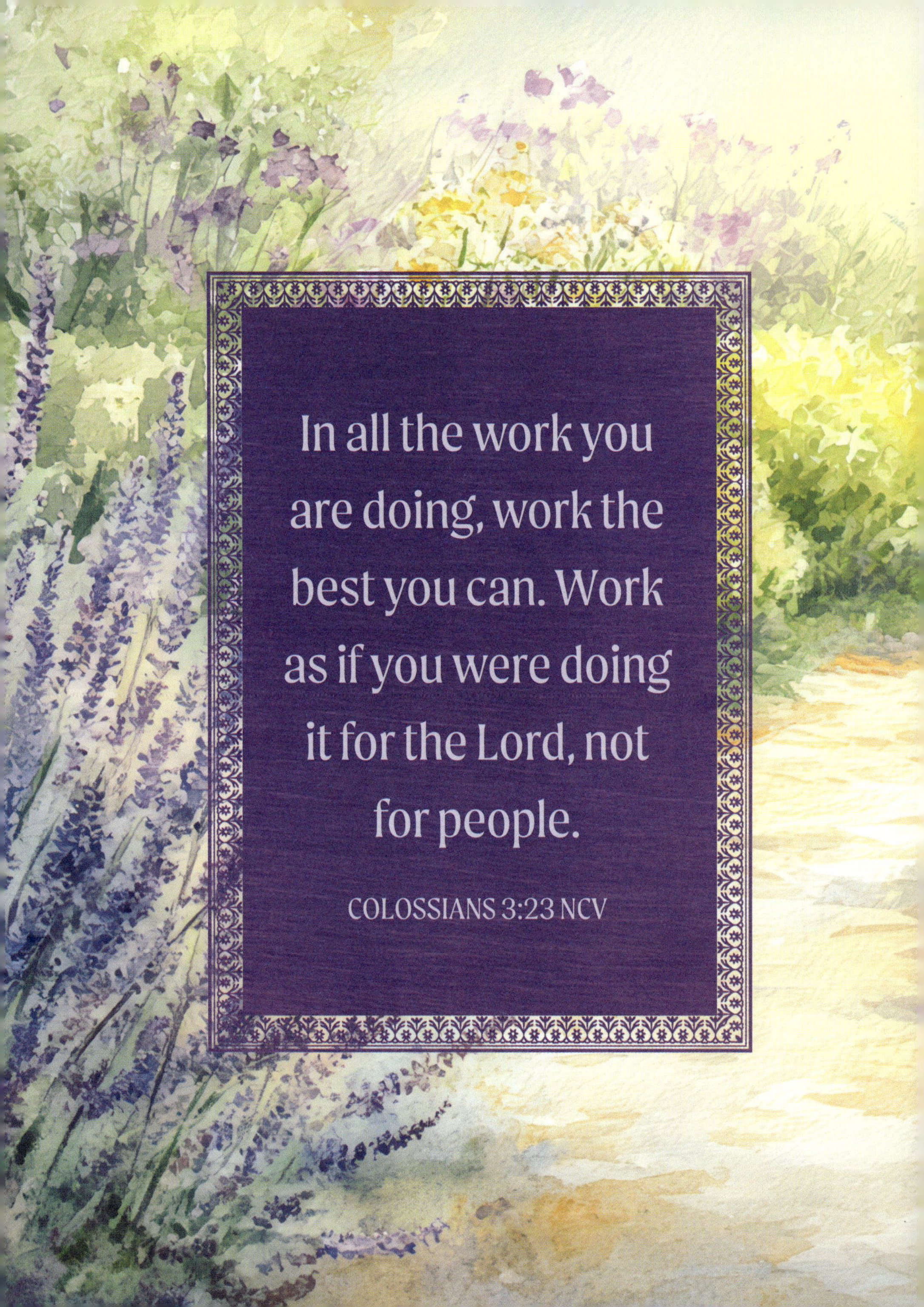
In all the work you are doing, work the best you can. Work as if you were doing it for the Lord, not for people.
COLOSSIANS 3:23 NCV

The Work of My Hands

What was your very first job? How did you get it?

How did your first paycheck make you feel, and how did you spend it?

Did you have a job when you were in high school?

What did your early jobs teach you about responsibility, effort, or money?

Did you have a dream job or fantasy of what you wanted to be when you grew up?

Who influenced or inspired your career path?

How did your education shape the path you took in life?

How did you choose your career?

What was your favorite job, and why?

What coworkers were most memorable?

Did you ever change directions in your career, and why or why not?

What job did you most dislike? What did you learn from it?

What was a typical workday like for you?

What accomplishments at work made you most proud?

What challenges or setbacks did you face, and how did you overcome them?

A man who wants to lead the orchestra must turn his back on the crowd.

MAX LUCADO

How did your work shape your confidence?

What did work teach you about people?

What was the hardest lesson you learned on the job?

How did you learn to balance work with family or personal life?

What do you think was your greatest contribution through your work?

If you could have pursued any career without limits, what would it have been?

What passions or talents did you get to use in your work life?

Which gifts do you think were left untapped?

Who was your favorite boss, and why?

Was there a comment made during a review that stuck with you? What was it?

What did you love the most about your job?

What three words would you use to describe your work ethic?

What might life have looked like if you had taken a job you passed on?

If you could give your children one piece of advice about work, what would it be?

What do you hope others remember about you as a worker, coworker, or leader?

What was your longest held job, and why did you stay?

Was your integrity ever put to the test at work, and how did you respond?

What role did faith play in the way you approached your work?

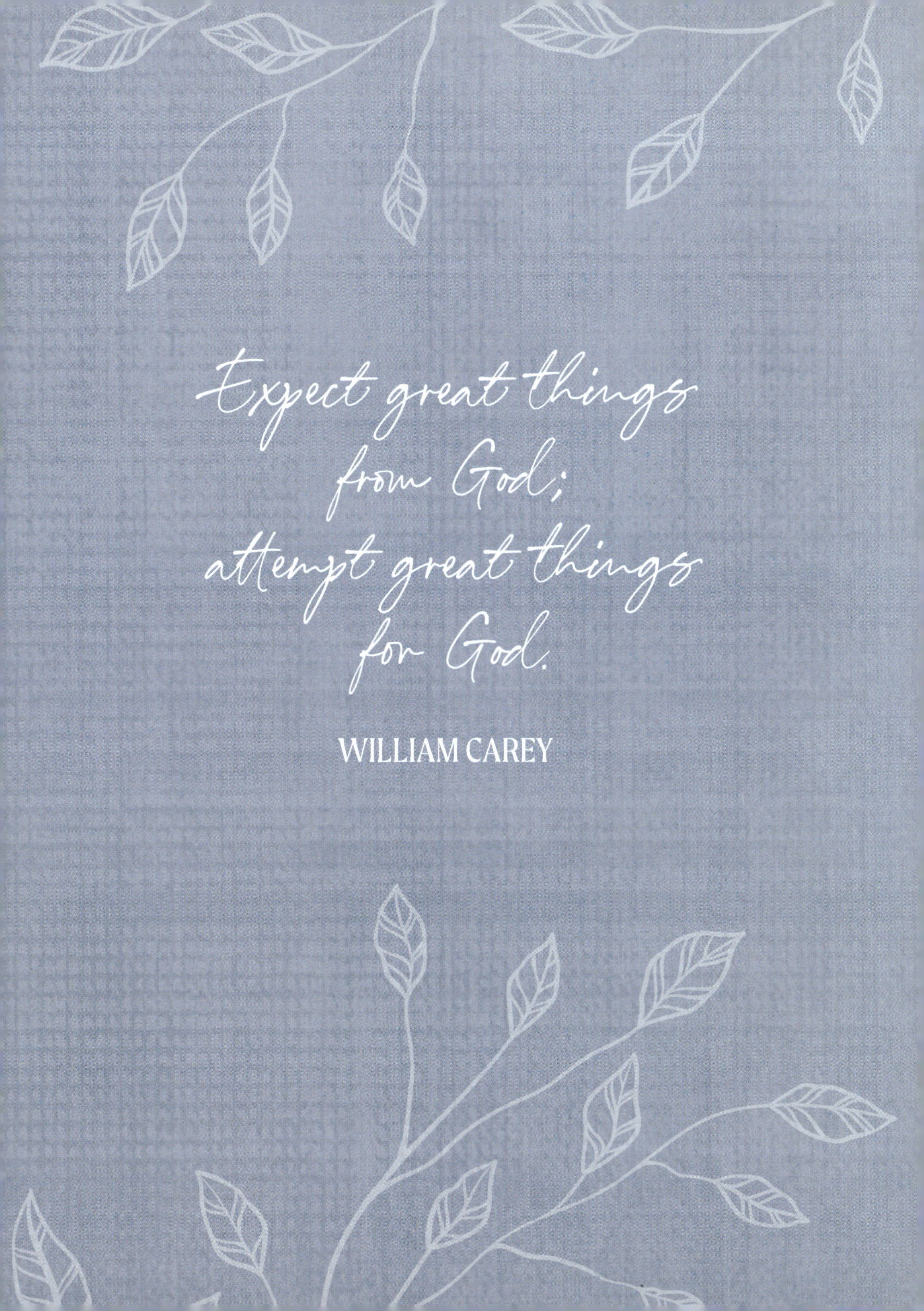
Expect great things
from God;
attempt great things
for God.
WILLIAM CAREY

Through the Senses

What did your office or workspace look like?

What sounds do you specifically remember at your workplace?

What scent greeted you each day when you arrived at work?

Where did you eat lunch most often?

What textures remind you of your work?

What object symbolizes your working years?

Significant Work

"The LORD has chosen Bezalel... and he has filled him with the Spirit of God, with wisdom, with understanding, with knowledge and with all kinds of skills—to make artistic designs for work in gold, silver and bronze, to cut and set stones, to work in wood."

EXODUS 35:30-33 NIV

Some jobs sure seem more important than others, like being a police officer or a doctor or a pilot. After all, police officers protect people, doctors save lives, and hundreds of people rely on a pilot's skill. What about being a pastor? Pastors tell people about God and help them understand the Bible. What's more important than that?

God chose a guy named Bezalel to create works of gold, silver, bronze, stone, and wood for the tabernacle: a place of worship. Then God filled him up with the power and creativity of his very own Spirit—not to preach, not to sing, but to build and make beautiful. The Creator himself gives special gifts of creativity—like writing, designing, and painting. He also gives gifts of administration, leadership, teaching, engineering, and many many more. Because these are all gifts from him, they are significant. He will give you all that you need to do your job well. You just have to ask.

How has God empowered you to do the jobs he has set before you? How do you use your talents for him?

May your hands always find purpose, and your labor be blessed with meaning.

The things
I loved to do in
my free time
reflect the joys
God placed in
my heart.

CHAPTER 4

Leisure & Interests

Every good and
perfect gift is from
above, coming
down from the
Father of the
heavenly lights,
who does not
change like shifting
shadows.
JAMES 1:17 NIV

My Passions and Pastimes

What did you collect, if anything, as a child, teen, or adult?

What hobbies or activities did you most enjoy in your free time?

What books, shows, or movies were your favorites through the years?

What did "fun" look like for you when you were younger compared to now?

What pastime helped you relax or recharge?

What talents did you use for leisure?

Who introduced you to your favorite hobby?

How would you spend a day outdoors?

How would you spend a day indoors?

Did you travel or dream about traveling? Where did you go or want to go?

What is your favorite travel memory?

What causes, volunteer work, or community services were you passionate about?

Did you prefer to do things by yourself or with others, and why?

Which interests of yours became lifelong loves, and which were just a phase?

How did your interests help you through hard times?

You are never too old to set another goal or to dream a new dream.

C.S. LEWIS

What passion best represents who you are at your core?

How did you balance your leisure time with work and family life?

Did you ever imagine a completely different future for yourself, and if so, what?

Is there a talent or hobby that you wish you had developed further?

Which of your passions could you have turned into a career?

Are there any creative pursuits you wanted to try but never did?

What is one thing you wish you had made more time for?

If time and money were no object, what passion would you dive into today?

What object symbolizes your joy in your free time?

What did it feel like to finish something with your own hands?

What activity could you lose track of time doing?

Who, if anyone, did you enjoy your leisure activities with?

What passion or pastime has stayed with you the longest?

Did you ever teach your hobby to someone else?

What have your favorite pastimes taught you?

What would a perfect day look like to you?

What is your "superpower" (what do you do better than most people you know)?

What did your passions and pastimes teach you about yourself?

You have made us
for yourself, O Lord,
and our hearts are
restless until they
rest in you.
ST. AUGUSTINE

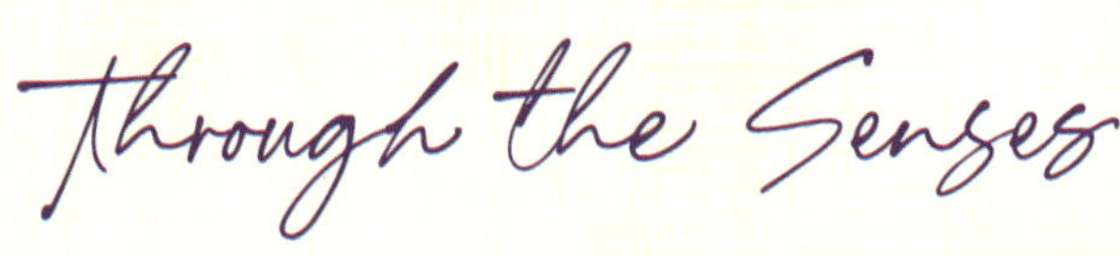

What did your favorite hobby space look like?

What sounds remind you of your favorite pastime?

What smell takes you back to your favorite hobby?

What kind of food goes along with your passion?

What tools most remind you of your favorite leisure activities?

What memory of "just having fun" makes you smile instantly?

Transferred Skills

God has given each of you a gift from his great variety of spiritual gifts. Use them well to serve one another.

1 Peter 4:10 NLT

Do you like to cook, garden, or play an instrument? If you think about things you enjoy, you can probably also trace them back to when you started to learn how to do them. God has gifted everyone with particular talents and skills, and it is our pleasure to be able to be taught, or to pass the skill along to others.

Thank Jesus for the gifts that you have received and are able to pass on. It is a joy when you see someone master something they didn't know how to do before and experience satisfaction when they have created something beautiful. The community of learning and passing it on is truly God inspired.

What things that you enjoy come with a natural talent or ability to excel in them? What would it look like to teach those skills to future generations?

May the passions
you pursued, whether
simple or grand,
inspire others to
discover the joy of
the talents and delights
God has placed within
each person.

My love story is
woven with grace,
commitment, and
the beauty of
walking hand
in hand.

CHAPTER 5
Love &
Marriage

Place me like a seal
over your heart,
like a seal on your arm.
For love is as strong as
death, its jealousy as
enduring as the grave.
Love flashes like fire,
the brightest kind of flame.
Many waters cannot
quench love, nor can
rivers drown it.
SONG OF SOLOMON 8:6-7 NLT

The Story of Us

When was your very first crush?

What did dating look like when you were a young adult?

What did your first serious relationship teach you?

How and when did you meet the person you ended up marrying?

What first attracted you to your husband?

What did you do on your first date?

When did you realize this man was "the one"?

How long did you date for, and what did you like to do the most together?

What do you remember about the proposal?

When and where did you get married?

Who were the most important people present at your wedding?

What did your dress look like?

How did your husband react when he first saw you in your dress?

Who were your bridesmaids, and why did you choose them?

What memorable moments, funny stories, or surprises were part of your wedding?

It is not your love that sustains the marriage, but from now on, the marriage that sustains your love.

DIETRICH BONHOEFFER

Where did you go on your honeymoon?

What was it like to begin married life together?

Where was your first home together?

What were the joys and challenges in the early years of marriage?

What has marriage taught you about partnership?

What has been your favorite part of married life?

What qualities have made your relationship strong?

If you could relive one day with your spouse, what day would it be?

What advice would you give others about marriage?

What have you learned about love over the years?

What particularly difficult challenge have you faced together?

What do or did you love the most about your husband?

What did you and your husband dream about in the early years of marriage?

What did you enjoy doing together in the later years of marriage?

What is your favorite way to make others feel loved?

What do you think is the best way to make big decisions?

What traits do you most value in your relationships?

How has marriage shaped the woman you are today?

Love feels no burden, thinks nothing of trouble, attempts what is above its strength. It pleads no excuse of impossibility; for it thinks all things lawful for itself, and all things possible.

THOMAS Á KEMPIS

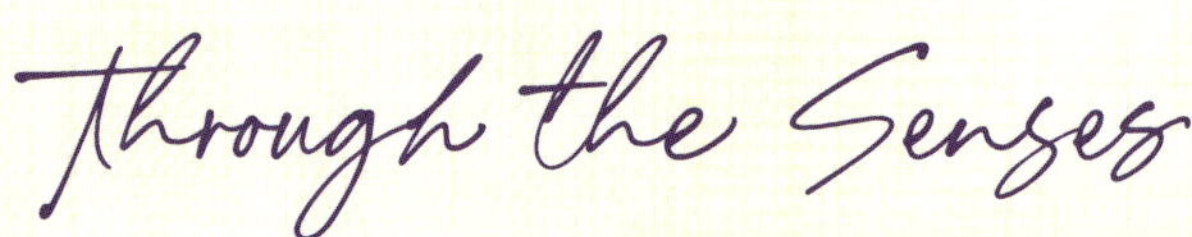

What is your favorite feature on your husband?

What song takes you instantly back to your courtship or wedding day?

Is there a fragrance that will always remind you of your husband?

What meal or specific food do you most enjoy together?

What do you remember about the first kiss with your husband?

What small, everyday gestures of love do you remember most clearly?

Prized and Respected

Marriage is to be honored by all and
the marriage bed kept undefiled.

Hebrews 13:4 CSB

In the beginning, God made marriage a very clear institution of his own design. One man and one woman came together for life, separating from their families and joining together to create a new family. Since then, we have messed with the design, trying to make it work with our own desires. We have taken marriage and devalued it, all the way back from the kings of Israel up to this generation today.

God never intended for marriage to be treated so poorly. It was to be held in high regard. God himself indicates his intention toward the Church is to cherish it like he does marriage. Marriage is a prized and respected concept in God's kingdom. As he esteems it, so should we. Let's bring value back to the institution of marriage as God originally designed it.

What does celebrating and encouraging the marriages around you look like? What have you done to honor your own marriage?

May your love story
remind others that
marriage is a covenant:
strengthened by
patience, softened by
grace, and made
steadfast through the
unfailing love of God.

Motherhood stretched my heart in ways I never imagined, teaching me both sacrifice and unshakable love.

CHAPTER 6
Motherhood

Start children off
on the way they
should go,
and even when
they are old they
will not turn from it.
PROVERBS 22:6 NIV

My Greatest Calling

How did you feel when you first found out you were going to be a mother?

How did you feel during pregnancy?

What funny stories do you have about your first pregnancy?

What do you remember most vividly about the day your first child was born?

How did you choose your children's names?

What surprised you most about becoming a mother?

What was life like with a newborn in the house?

What baby or toddler moments still make you smile?

What unexpected challenges did you encounter?

What routines became special in your family?

What did you love the most about watching your children grow?

What was it like raising children during their school years?

How did you celebrate birthdays, holidays, and milestones?

What were your proudest parenting moments?

What struggles or worries were especially hard to navigate?

No language can express the power and beauty and heroism of a mothers' love.

EDWIN HUBBELL CHAPIN

How did you balance parenting with work, marriage, and your own interests?

What has being a mother taught you about love?

What lessons have your children taught you?

Is being a mother what you expected it to be?

If you could do things differently as a parent, what would you do?

If a robot could take over one chore for you, what would it be?

What family traditions did you create that you hope will continue?

What parenting advice would you give to others?

What have you learned about yourself through being a mother?

What particularly difficult challenge have you faced in motherhood?

What three words most characterize you as a mother?

What do you hope your children remember about their childhood?

How is being a mother of adult children different for you?

What did you enjoy the most about your children becoming adults?

What do you love about being a mother?

How is each child like you, and how are they different?

If you could give one message to your children about your journey as their mother, what would it be?

How has being a mother shaped the woman you are today?

There is more power
in a mother's hand than
in a king's scepter.
BILLY SUNDAY

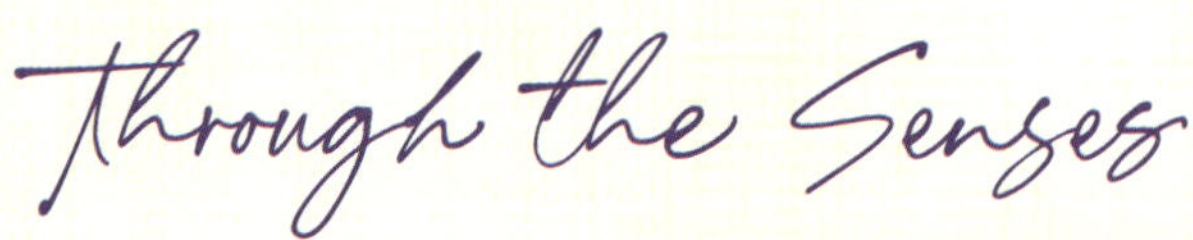

Which of your children looks like you? Who looks like your husband?

What kids' song, movie, or book do you most associate with your children?

What smell takes you back to parenting little ones?

What meal did your children get most excited about?

How did you show your children affection?

What moments, big or small, most capture the feeling of being a mother?

Confident Children

Because you are his sons, God sent the Spirit of his
Son into our hearts, the Spirit who calls out,
"Abba, Father."

Galatians 4:6 NIV

Children who know they are loved can go to their parents without fear of being shamed or ignored. Even if your natural family did not allow for this type of confident freedom, you have a perfect and loving heavenly Father who welcomes you whenever you come to him. You can approach him without fear, knowing how dearly loved you are.

Whenever you need your Father, he is near. When you call out to him, he hears you, answers you, and holds you close. You can trust that when you ask him for help, he will always move in faithfulness. His ways are far better than yours, so trust his love more than your dictation of happiness. He can handle you no matter what state you are in. You can freely and confidently come to him with everything.

Do you approach God as a confident child, knowing he loves you unconditionally? How have you tried to be like him in your relationship with your children?

May every moment
of sacrifice and joy
in motherhood
echo as a lasting
gift of love.

My faith and
values became
the compass that
guided me
through every
season of life.

CHAPTER 7

Faith & Values

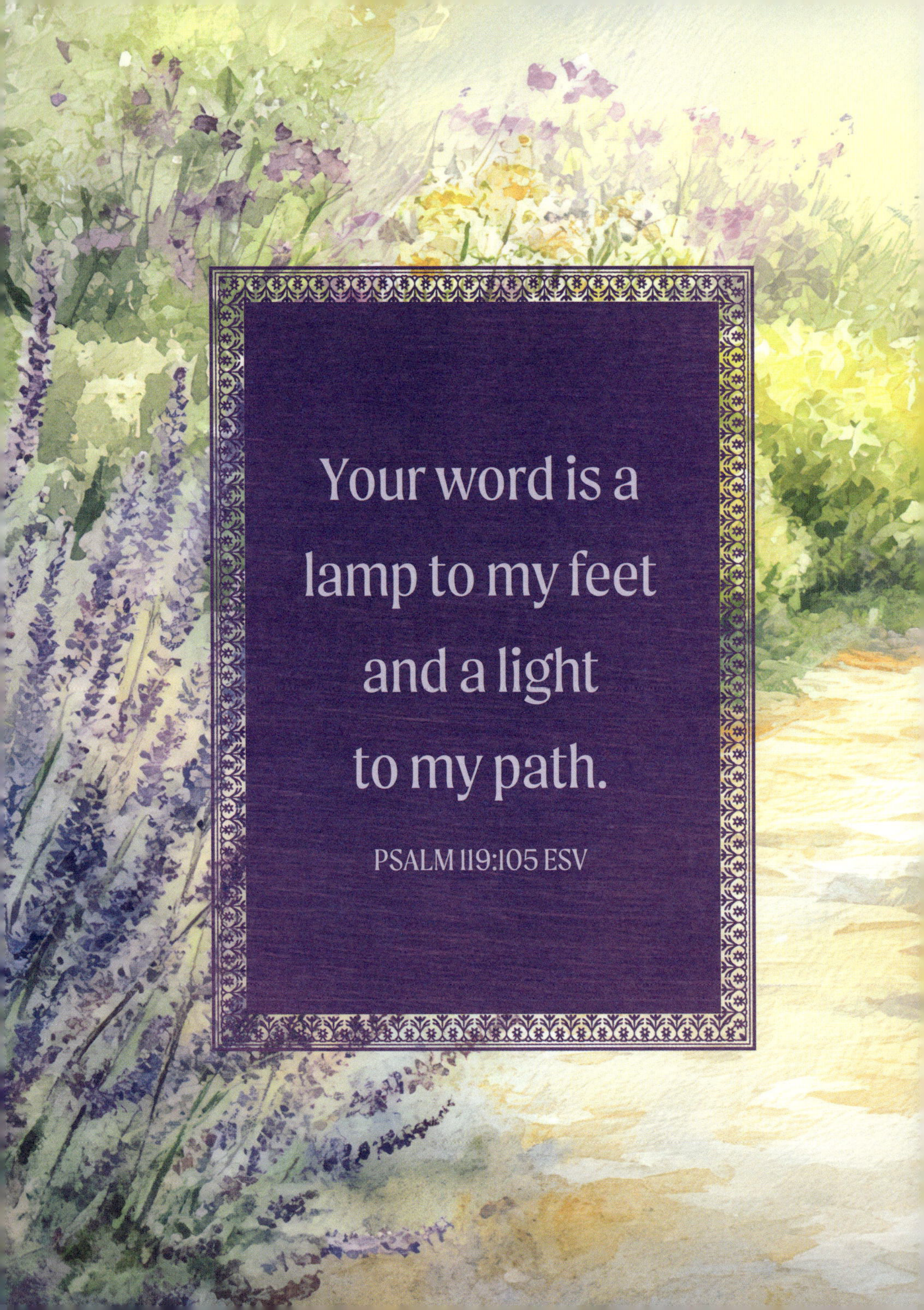
Your word is a
lamp to my feet
and a light
to my path.
PSALM 119:105 ESV

The Truth I Live By

When did faith first enter your life?

Who influenced your beliefs most when you were young?

What family traditions or rituals shaped your sense of values?

What role did church, prayer, or sacred practices play in your childhood?

What guiding principle did you carry with you from an early age?

How did your faith and values guide your choices in life?

How has your belief system been tested, and how did you respond?

What role did faith play in your marriage and parenting?

What principles and values do you try to model for your children?

What Christian holidays have you always celebrated, and what do they mean to you?

What is your favorite Bible story and why?

What truths or values have never wavered for you?

How has your worldview evolved over time?

What has brought you the most peace and assurance over the years?

What values do you most hope to pass on to your children and grandchildren?

The greatest legacy one can pass on to one's children and grandchildren is not money or other material things, but rather a legacy of character and faith.

BILLY GRAHAM

Have you ever questioned or wrestled with your faith?

What values do you wish you had lived out more fully?

How has your faith helped you face hardship?

What is your favorite Bible verse?

What do you believe about the character of God?

What character of God do you find fascinating?

If you could talk to one person in the Bible, who would it be and why?

How have you tried to live out your faith in daily life?

What ministry or Christian service have you been involved in over the years?

What value have you found especially difficult to live out?

How has your faith deepened over the years?

If you could pass on three values to future generations, what would they be?

Where do you go to find peace when anxiety threatens to overwhelm you?

What do you pray over your family regularly?

If you could write a one-sentence life motto, what would it be?

What do you think is the purpose of life?

How have you seen the faithfulness of God through the years?

What spiritual dream do you hold for your family?

God is most glorified
in us when we are
most satisfied in him.
JOHN PIPER

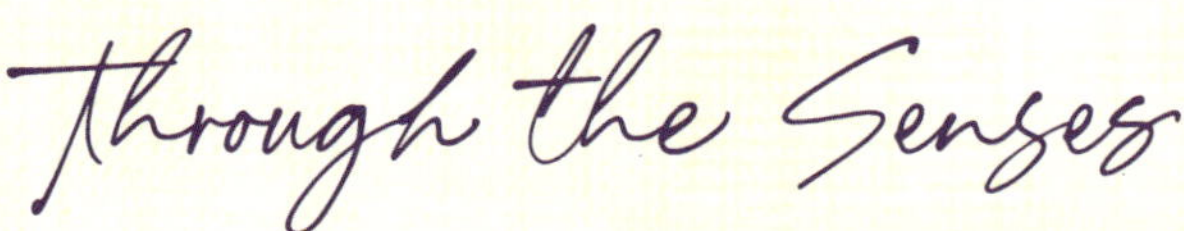

What beauty in nature most reminds you of the awesomeness of God?

What worship song resounds with you most?

What smells remind you of family traditions tied to your faith?

When have you tasted the goodness of God?

When have you most felt the presence of God?

When you think of your walk with God, what memories bring back the peace, joy, or comfort of his presence?

Growing Deeper

May God give you more and more grace and peace as you grow in your knowledge of God and Jesus our Lord.

2 PETER 1:2 NLT

The fear of failure is one of life's biggest struggles. Failure is not a great feeling, and yet most successful people will tell you that failure has been a part of their experience. There is something to be said for the knowledge that comes from experience. As your experience of God grows, your understanding of simple concepts like peace and grace will develop into deep truths.

The knowledge of God is not a test you can fail. Every new thing you learn about Christ will add to your faith. Climb the mountains of life with him, test him at his Word, and find his promises to be true. As you explore the truth, your preconceived notions of peace and grace may be challenged. Treasure this deeper understanding in your heart. God will show you the purest forms of the most wonderful things. Ask him to reveal himself to you, and experience the joy of discovering a life of fullness in him.

How has your faith deepened as you've walked with God?

May your steps
always be guided
by God's light,
and your heart
remain anchored
in the truth.

the things I
cherished most
may seem simple,
but together they
paint a picture
of who I am.

CHAPTER 8

Favorites

"If you then, who are evil, know how to give good gifts to your children, how much more will your Father in heaven give good things to those who ask him."
MATTHEW 7:11 CSB

A Few of My Favorite Things

What five foods could you never resist?

What was your favorite food growing up?

What are five songs you'd never skip?

Who is your favorite music artist?

What childhood book still makes you smile?

What five books would you recommend to anyone?

What are your five favorite movies or TV shows?

What movie have you watched the most?

What are five places you've loved visiting?

What five places would you like to visit?

Has your favorite color changed over the years?

What favorite thing of yours do you hope your children will try or like one day?

What is your favorite sports team, and why?

What five things always make you laugh?

What small thing makes you happy?

Mountaintops are for views and inspiration, but fruit is grown in the valleys.

BILLY GRAHAM

What are five of your pet peeves?

If you could spend the day with one famous person, who would it be and why?

What are your top five little luxuries (things that make life easier)?

What is your favorite time of day, and why?

What is one thing you love that people may not know about?

Of the following, what would you prefer?

❏ Coffee ❏ Tea

❏ Sweet ❏ Salty

❏ Chocolate ❏ Vanilla

❏ Pizza ❏ Burgers

❏ Steak ❏ Salad

❏ Ice cream ❏ Milkshake

❏ Homemade meal ❏ Eating out

❏ Book ❏ Movie

❏ Comedy ❏ Drama

❏ Dancing ❏ Singing

❏ Board game ❏ Card game

❏ Cozy night in ❏ Night on the town

❏ Art gallery ❏ Concert

❏ Shoes ❏ Barefoot

❏ Jeans ❏ Sweats

❑ Gold ❑ Silver

❑ Adventure ❑ Relaxation

❑ Road trip ❑ Flying

❑ Beach vacation ❑ Mountain getaway

❑ Dogs ❑ Cats

❑ Fruit ❑ Vegetables

❑ Summer ❑ Winter

❑ Rainy day ❑ Snowy day

❑ Sunrise ❑ Sunset

❑ Morning ❑ Night

❑ City lights ❑ Country skies

❑ Plan ahead ❑ Go with the flow

❑ Wrapped gift ❑ Gift card

❑ DIY ❑ Hire someone

❑ Save ❑ Spend

Top 40

Favorite color

Favorite number

Favorite flower

Favorite season

Favorite animal

Favorite place in nature

Favorite vacation spot

Favorite city

Favorite country

Favorite scent

Favorite restaurant

Favorite menu item

Favorite recipe

Favorite pizza topping

Favorite ice cream flavor

Favorite fruit

Favorite dessert

Favorite snack

Favorite candy

Favorite drink

Favorite song

Favorite band

Favorite instrument

Favorite sound

Favorite phrase

Favorite article of clothing

Favorite sport

Favorite hobby

Favorite car

Favorite day of the week

Favorite holiday

Favorite tradition

Favorite teacher

Favorite subject

Favorite book

Favorite game

Favorite TV show

Favorite movie

Favorite male actor

Favorite female actor

Why do you think your favorite things bring you so much joy?

What are your favorite qualities about yourself?

What do you think God's favorite thing about you is?

Joy is the serious business of heaven.
C.S. LEWIS

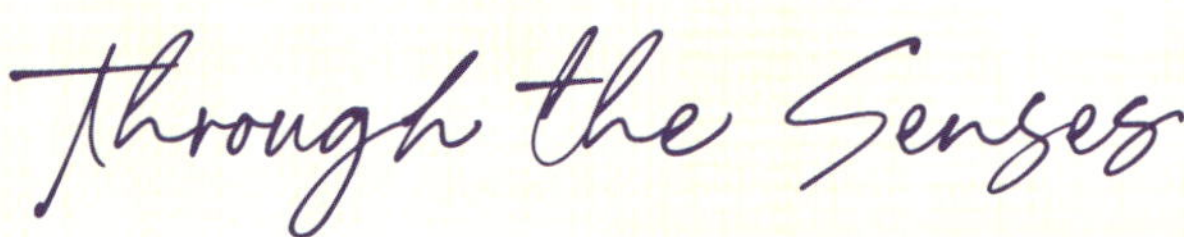

What image or scene, when you picture it in your mind, still makes you smile?

What sound makes you instantly happy?

What is your favorite fragrance?

What is your go-to flavor?

What textures bring back good memories?

If someone created a “Favorites” box to remember you by, what five things would go inside it?

Delighting in Details

The LORD directs the steps of the godly.
He delights in every detail of their lives.
Though they stumble, they will never fall,
for the LORD holds them by the hand.

PSALM 37:23-24 NLT

Imagine a father walking hand-in-hand with his toddler, his steps steady and even, the toddler wobbly and still a little unsure on her feet. He keeps his eyes on the child, making sure she won't fall. The child excitedly points out everything that delights her. A leaf! A bug! A flower! And with each minute observation, the father smiles because his delight is in his child. He is not too old, too mature, or too grown to brush past what is important to his daughter in that moment.

This is the type of father you have. He delights in every detail of your life. Nothing about your day, even though he has seen millions of days, is too minute for him. Nothing about your life is too insignificant. He delights in every little part of you. He holds you firmly, so you won't fall, and he directs your steps because he cares for you. Share the mundane and the small with him. He wants to meet you in your big difficult moments, but he also wants to join you in the seemingly insignificant ones.

How does it make you feel to think of God as being close and personal, concerned with the details of your days? How can you invite him into every aspect of your life?

May the simple delights of life remind you that God's goodness is everywhere.

Wisdom is the gift I can give that will outlast me, carried forward in the choices you make.

CHAPTER 9

Words of Wisdom

Blessed are those
who find wisdom,
those who gain
understanding,
for she is more
profitable than silver
and yields better
returns than gold.
PROVERBS 3:13-14 NIV

My Life Reflections

What have you learned that you wish you would have understood sooner in life?

What has love taught you?

What has loss taught you?

What moments of failure turned out to be blessings in disguise?

What values have guided you most strongly through life?

What decisions in life are you happy you made?

What things would you do differently?

How do you think someone should choose a career or path in life?

What would you tell people about love and marriage?

What advice would you give someone about raising children?

How have your friendships and relationships with others shaped you?

What do you think is the best way to handle challenges or setbacks?

What brings about true happiness?

What life hack do you frequently use or tell people about?

What is your attitude toward money and financial wealth?

Prayer does not fit us
for the greater work;
prayer is the greater work.

OSWALD CHAMBERS

How would you define success?

What has been your biggest fear, and how have you overcome it?

If you could go back and talk to your younger self, what would you say?

If you had taken a different path in life, what might you have missed out on?

What do you still hope to learn?

What legacy of wisdom do you most want your children to carry forward?

What is your favorite proverb and why?

What have you learned about forgiveness?

In what moments have you had to choose gratitude?

What do you find yourself saying over and over again?

If you knew today was your last day, how would you spend it?

What is the best advice you've ever been given?

Who do you most often go to for advice, and why?

What is most important in a life well lived?

What do you want to be remembered for?

What is the hardest thing you've ever been through, and how did you persevere?

If you could encourage other generations to do one thing like your generation, what would it be?

Where do you think wisdom comes from, and how do you pursue it?

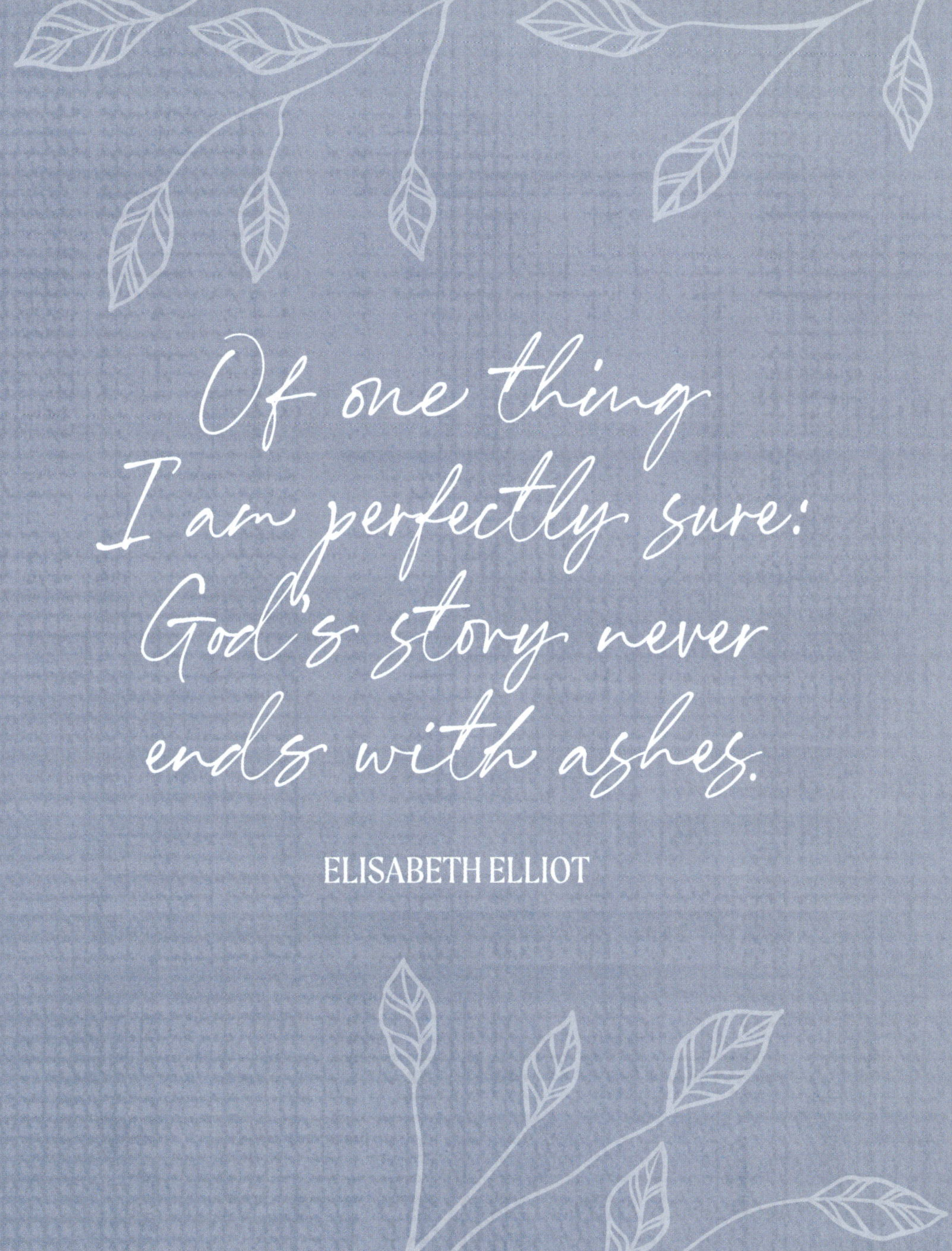

Of one thing
I am perfectly sure:
God's story never
ends with ashes.

ELISABETH ELLIOT

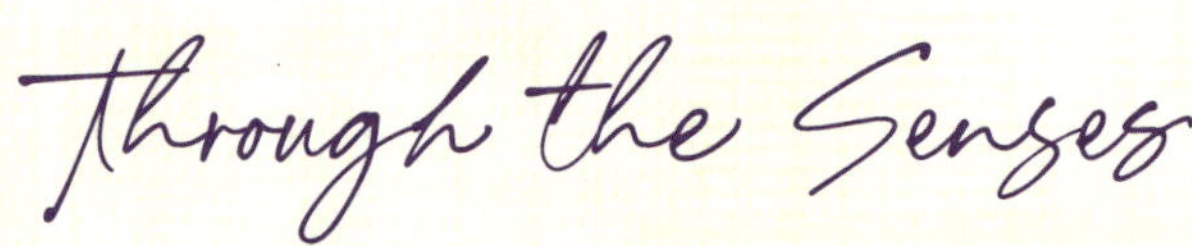

Whose example has taught you the most about living well?

What words of wisdom do you live by?

What kind of aroma do you hope to spread to others?

What morsel of wisdom has been sweeter than honey to you?

What simple object reminds you of wisdom passed down?

If you could summarize your life philosophy in one sentence, what would it be, and why?

Chase Wisdom

Teach the wise, and they will become even wiser;
teach good people, and they will learn even more.

Proverbs 9:9 NCV

The moment a person decides they can't learn anything from someone else is the moment they stop learning at all. It is openness to being taught that makes you wise. The wisest people never stop learning, never stop exploring, seeing, or doing. They have an insatiable hunger to be taught. They understand that they are not the experts on everything and that there is always a person with more experience, more knowledge, and more passion.

Never close yourself off to learning something new—not even from those younger than you. In moments of frustration or failure, you can learn. Learn to lead; learn to love. Explore with eagerness. Learn from your triumphs and celebrate small victories. Rejoice in the lifelong education of doing life with others. Chase wisdom and never assume you have arrived at obtaining it.

In what ways have you chased wisdom?

May your words
live on as
seeds of wisdom,
planted deep
in the hearts of
those you love.

These notes are more than words; they are reminders of my love. Here I share not just memories, but blessings, hopes, and prayers for those I hold dearest.

CHAPTER 10

Notes to Loved Ones

Every time I
think of you,
I give thanks
to my God.
PHILIPPIANS 1:3 NLT

Letters from My Heart

The next pages are a place for you to write words to specific people or groups of people. Here are some ideas to consider that might help you leave a special message for the ones you love.

To My Spouse

Tell how your love story has shaped your life.

Share gratitude for everyday moments that made your marriage strong.

Express what you admire most about them.

To My Children

Say what they mean to you.

Share a memory of them that makes you smile every time you think of it.

Tell them what you hope they will always remember about your love.

To My Grandchildren or Future Generations

Write about who you are and what you believe.

Share a word of wisdom that you hope they carry forward.

Tell them what you dream for them.

To My Parents

Say what you learned from them that helped carry you through life.

Write a favorite memory that still warms your heart.

Express what you're most grateful for in how they raised you.

To Those I've Lost

Say what you wish you could tell them today.

Share how their influence lives on in you.

Write about what you miss the most and what you carry forward.

Writing Starters

I want you to know…

My favorite memory with you is…

I admire you because…

I will always carry this about you in my heart…

If I could give you one gift for life, it would be…

Feed your fears, and your faith will starve. Feed your faith, and your fears will.

MAX LUCADO

NOTES TO LOVED ONES

Worry does not empty
tomorrow of its sorrow.
It empties today of its strength.

CORRIE TEN BOOM

May these words
carry the echo of love,
spoken once and
remembered forever.

Every story has more to tell,
but some memories and feelings
don't fit neatly into chapters.
The next pages are for the overflow—
share whatever is left on your heart.

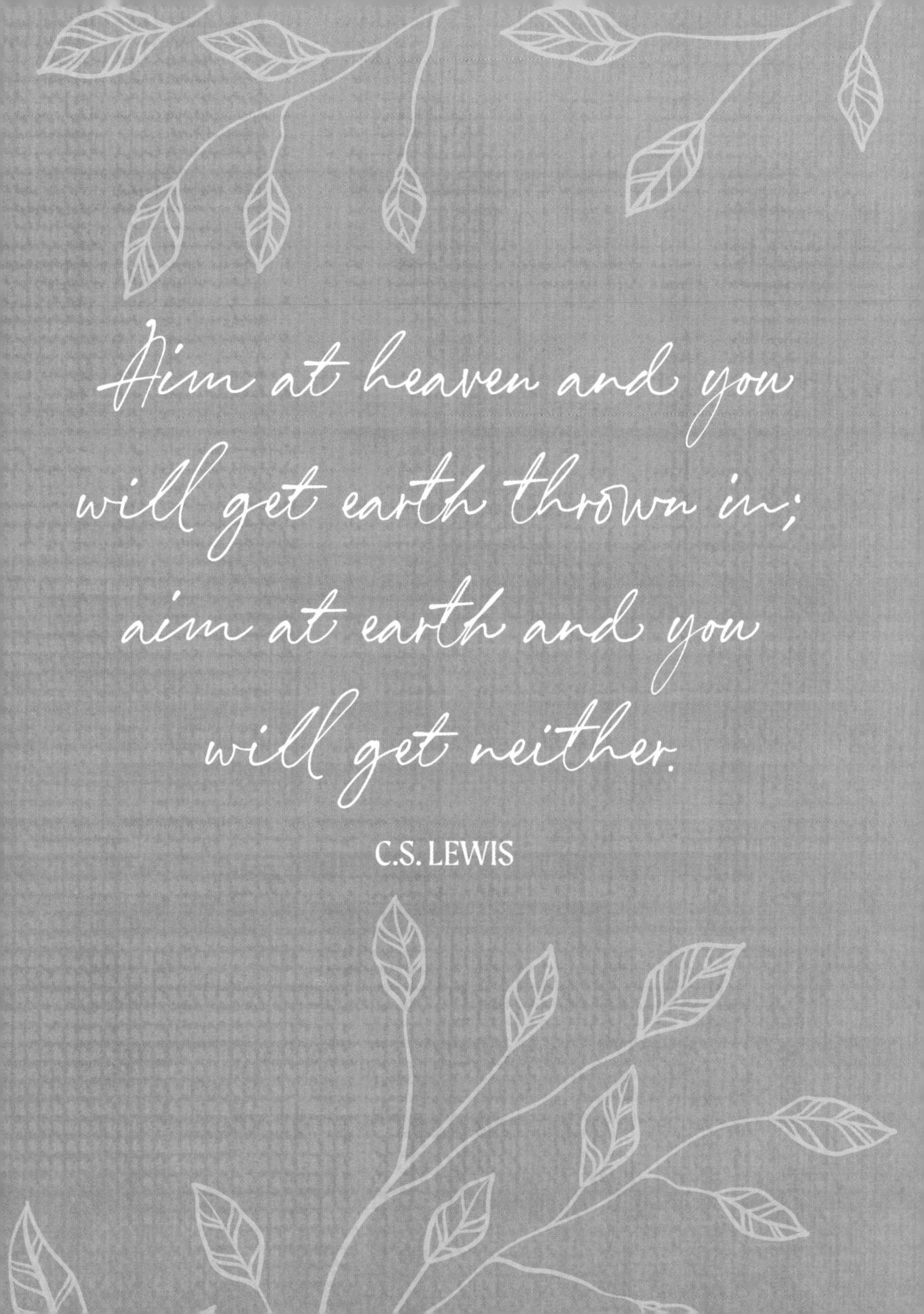
Aim at heaven and you
will get earth thrown in;
aim at earth and you
will get neither.
C.S. LEWIS

Closing Words

As these pages close, my hope is not only that you know my story,
but that you also see the hand of God woven through every chapter.
The joys and the struggles, the blessings and the lessons—
all of them were shaped by his love and grace.

I pray you carry this truth with you:
that you are wonderfully made, deeply loved, and never alone.
God's faithfulness is everlasting,
and his promises will carry you through every season of life.

When you walk in doubt, lean on his Word.
When you feel weary, trust his strength.
When anxiety creeps in, place your hope in him.
When you notice his blessings, give him thanks.

My greatest legacy is not in what I've done,
but in passing on the faith that has sustained me.
May you always know the hope found in Christ,
the peace that comes from his Spirit,
and the love of a Father who will never let you go.

With all my love and prayers.

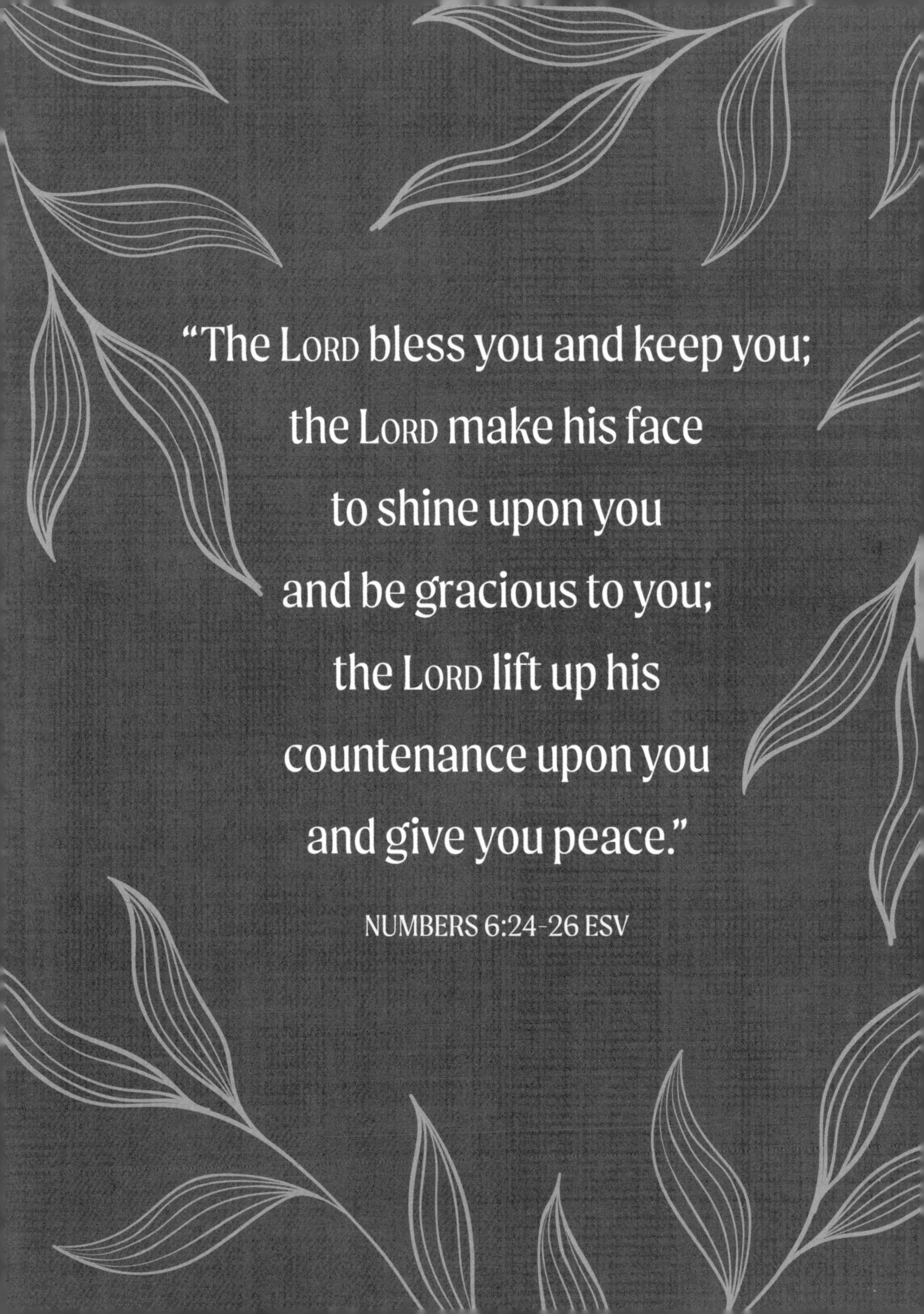
"The LORD bless you and keep you;
the LORD make his face
to shine upon you
and be gracious to you;
the LORD lift up his
countenance upon you
and give you peace."
NUMBERS 6:24-26 ESV